Tiny
TIM AND
GHOST THE OST
of Ebenezer Scrooge

Tiny TIM AND GHOST THE OST

of Ebenezer Scrooge

New Christmas Carols Inside!

The sequel to A Christmas Carol

Norman Whaler

Tiny Tim and The Ghost of Ebenezer Scrooge
The sequel to A Christmas Carol

Beneath Another Sky Books
Copyright © 2018 by Norman Whaler.

Based on A Christmas Carol by Charles Dickens.

Book design copyright © 2018 by Norman Whaler.
All rights reserved.
Cover art by Stewart Sherwood
Cover design by Niño Carlo Suico
Interior design by Suzette Vaughn
Editor for UK English by Jools Bond
Music copyright © Norman Whaler

Library of Congress Catalogue Number: 2017916356

ISBN Hardcover: 978-1-948131-00-1
ISBN Paperback: 978-1-948131-02-5
ISBN ePub: 978-1-948131-01-8
ISBN Kindle: 978-1-948131-06-3

normanwhaler.com

And the ones on the rock are those who,
when they hear the word, receive it with joy.
But these have no root; they believe for a while,
and in time of testing fall away.
—Luke 8:13

I have said these things to you,
that in me you may have peace. In the world you will have
tribulation. But take heart; I have overcome the world."
—John 16:33

Fear not, for I am with you; be not dismayed,
for I am your God; I will strengthen you,
I will help you, I will uphold you
with my righteous right hand.
—Isaiah 41:10

For my wife, Patricia, who passed on Nov 19, 2011.

Honey, I love you more every day. I thank God for His grace and for every moment He gave me with you.

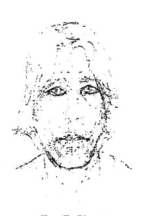

Tiny Tim Cratchit

Contents

Illustrations

PROLOGUE

What Went Before

December, 1857
Christmas time, London

The sign above the warehouse door was weatherworn and faded, but could still be easily read — Scrooge & Marley & Cratchit. The '& Cratchit' could be seen to be an addition to the original sign because of the clarity of letters and the way they were crowded on a descending angle in the small space left over after the name 'Marley'.

In the beginning, the offices had been those of Ebenezer Scrooge and his business partner, Jacob Marley. Cratchit was added to the sign some seven years after Marley's death, but the original sign was never repainted nor was Marley's name deleted. The firm was now known as Scrooge & Marley & Cratchit. This did make for some confusion to those new to the business who called Cratchit "Cratchit," or sometimes "Marley" or "Scrooge," but being a good and humble man, Cratchit answered to all three so as not to embarrass.

Bob Cratchit had been a clerk to both Scrooge and Marley (before Marley passed from the mortal) and had become a junior partner with Scrooge in the firm fourteen years ago. Now, just seven days before Christmas, he is a full partner with Scrooge's nephew, Fred, following Scrooge's death.

STAVE 1

Scrooge is Dead

Yes! Old Scrooge is DEAD, to begin with. I swear to it or I wouldn't be telling you of it right now. Old Scrooge is dead as a mackerel. Understand, I'm not telling you I know anything about why a mackerel is most always described as deceased, but when they make their appearance on my dinner plate, this has always been their physical condition, So, my statement, "Dead as a mackerel!" stands. This, I pray, you accept as true so something wonderful can come of the story you are about to hear.

Tiny Tim Cratchit, Bob Cratchit's lame little son, and old Scrooge had been inseparable. Ever since that time when Scrooge had befriended his clerk's little boy when he had almost died, they were never far apart. Scrooge, in fact, was like a second father to Tim, close after his beloved real father, Bob. You could even say that Tim owed his sturdy, healthy body and life to this man, Scrooge, who, at one time, had been a self-centred "hand at the grindstone Scrooge." Oh, yes! He had been "a squeezing, wrenching, grasping, scraping, clutching, covetous old sinner, hard and sharp as flint, from which no steel had ever struck out generous fire."

But, late in his years, Scrooge had experienced a miraculous change in his attitude about life and had become the most thoughtful, kind, caring, giving, generous, and loving benefactor "as the good old city knew, or any other good old city, town, or borough, in the good old world."

But, now after a long life, here he lay, the candles at both ends of his coffin flickering, agitated by the wind blowing through the cracks in the windows. His casket was plain in keeping with one step above pauper — this had been Scrooge's wish when he had made his own arrangements for his funeral some time ago. "Nothing fancy, mind, just anything will do," he had told the undertaker at the time.

Here then was Scrooge, his white hair glistening on his head and brow above a timeworn face of cavernous folds. In repose, Scrooge had a peaceful, unconcerned look that might well be said to be angelic. His hands were folded upon his chest, and from the doorway of the room, he had the appearance that he was merely asleep or praying before Morph pheus overtook him.

As yet, no one had come to visit Scrooge, but this was because the undertaker had two customers that very afternoon and one casket for them both. Scrooge, having passed later than the first and second in line, had to wait until a casket could be found for him. After all, it was first-come, first-served.

Now, through the frosted pane of the undertaker's front window, a face appeared — unmistakably, Bob Cratchit. After gazing for a time as though he were in deep thought, Cratchit disappeared and presently the front door agonised on its hinges followed by the sound of footsteps coming down the hall to where Ebenezer lay. Cratchit stopped in the doorway almost as if he expected the man in the casket across the room to bid him enter. Then, after a few more moments of hesitation, he walked slowly over to the side of Scrooge's bier and gazed thoughtfully down at him.

Immediately, warm memories of Scrooge flooded Cratchit's mind as he looked into Scrooge's gentle face and remembered back to when Tiny Tim would hobble on his one little crutch through the snows of winter to Scrooge's waiting arms, and later on when Tiny Tim was no longer crippled, the old man watching him slide on the ice at Cornhill, shouting encouragement, and clapping his hands in delight at the sight of it.

Cratchit was brought back to the present abruptly when the front door again groaned and slow approaching footsteps could be heard on the bare floor of the hallway. They stopped just before the opening into the room and no one appeared. Cratchit waited with expectation wondering for a moment if he had imagined the whole thing. But, then in the gloom a slight young man could be seen framed by the doorway. The handsome face etched in sorrow was Tiny Tim's. He just stood there motionless in this setting of finality, his eyes fixed on the casket of his friend, Mr. Scrooge. Then, after what seemed like a compassionate amount of time for Tim to adjust to the reality of the scene, Bob Cratchit held out his hand to his son and urged him gently, "Come on, Tim, come over here with us now."

Tim moved slowly over to the casket and looked down into Scrooge's peaceful face. It all seemed so unfair, so unreal, as if at any moment old Scrooge would awaken and they would be together again laughing and hugging each other as they so often did.

After a few more consoling moments, Cratchit moved quietly from beside Scrooge's coffin leaving his son alone there with his thoughts. Tim stood there for a long while and then, in a gesture of love, placed his hand on the clasped hands of Ebenezer. Almost in an instant, he was back again as a little boy with his small hand in Scrooge's huge hand, walking along in the snow, laughing and happy. But, now all of that was gone and he knew it would never come again.

"No! It isn't fair!" cried Tim, turning to his father sitting in a chair that had been provided for a visitor. "It isn't fair! It isn't fair, Father!" Tim repeated with tears welling up in his eyes. With that, he abruptly bolted from the room leaving his father alone there with Scrooge.

Outside and down the street he ran, passing Christmas carollers singing, "♫ *Have a Very-Very Merry-Merry Christmas* ♫," and little men and women with horns and drums adding their all to the Christmas celebration. Finally, Tim reached home and took his sorrow to bed.

"♫ *Have a Very-Very Merry-Merry Christmas* ♫"

Meanwhile, at this very same time on a busy street in London's old market, Becky, a very determined young lady and Tiny Tim's school sweetheart, is doing her best to sell sprigs of holly to people hurrying by, many with their faces turned down from the wind and snow.

She has been standing out in the cold now for hours with only a worn-thin shawl around her shoulders to protect her from the winter and patiently looking into each passing face and asking, "A bit of holly for your Christmas?"

Becky suddenly glanced down at her tattered dress and realised she had been unsuccessful at hiding a tear she had discovered that morning as she was getting dressed. She was mortified and embarrassed. For the thousandth time she asked herself why she had fallen so far. She simply did not know.

First, one thing had gone wrong in her life. Then another. And another. As well-to-do ladies and gentlemen continued to walk past, many averted their eyes and pretended not to notice her shabbiness. Some would even casually cross the road so they would not have to pass her on the pavement and speak to her. But, the worst were those who, with upturned noses, would openly display their disgust and disdain with cutting remarks making it quite clear to all their feelings on the matter of her presence in *their* street. As she stood in the middle of the pavement, for a small moment, the hurtful voices faded as Becky slipped into another world of her own thoughts.

Becky and Tim

At one time, she had been very happy. Although it was less than a decade ago, Becky remembered it like a caress. But, the young man she so deeply loved was not suitable for her rich high-society family and they demanded she forget her feelings for him. But, Becky never did. She remembered the words she had often spoken to him:

> *"Except for the times I breathe in,*
> *I think of you only when I breathe out..."*

Now, after the distance of all these years, Becky sadly wondered if she ever crossed his mind. But, being brought up in a proper home, and believing and living the Christian tenet of 'Honour the authors of thy being, thy Father and thy Mother,' Becky was finally forced to agree to her family's wishes for an arranged marriage to a successful, but older man she did not love. So that she would not have a chance to change her mind, her family whisked her away to their summer home up north to be married and away from any temptation to rashness.

Her new husband was, at first, a good and kindly man, but poor business decisions had begun to change him. As their fortunes had dwindled, so had his affections for his young wife and new-born son, James. As the years wore on, her husband's kindness had turned to bitterness, then to anger, and finally to rage.

"Come here, girl..." he would often say before his hand would fly. "Take your medicine as you should. I shan't ask you twice."

Becky often took days to recover and once it was more than a week. She couldn't understand why there weren't any responses from the letters sent home to her family, and her husband feigned any knowledge as to why this would be. Then, one night, Becky saw all her letters opened and read in the hands of her husband. He didn't speak and stared at her in a silence that frightened her as never before.

"Where's James?" he now asked casually, which was cruelly at odds with his soulless and unblinking gaze that froze her heart and pinned her to the floor where she stood.

As she realised his anger was beginning to focus on her little boy, Becky took her son and fled in the middle of the night whilst her husband was asleep. Knowing he would be quickly notified by the stable hands if she tried to have the use of a carriage or even a horse, Becky decided to walk the 11 miles to town in the downpour of the rain that had started late that evening. She felt danger pressing her from all sides and she needed to act if she were to save their lives.

Soaked to the skin by the unrelenting rain despite her attempts to keep dry, and having to carry little Jimmy, Becky staggered through the English muck and mire, bloodied by her falls on the hard stones in her path. The fierce wind forced the trees into a frenzied dance and their branches groaned and swayed violently as if imploring the furious storm to abate its wrath. Paranoia forced her to look constantly over her shoulder and angry lightning presented malevolent creatures of shadows that seemed all too real to her panicked senses.

The Storm

After several miles, she was exhausted and needed to rest, but the fear of being caught drove her insanely on. Then, in a moment of lucid clarity, the realisation came to her that she and Jimmy might not make it through the night and her courage stumbled. The storm's rage repeatedly assailed her, mocking her weakness, screaming at her that she could not win, beating her down into the hard bones of the earth.

The weight of their rain-soaked clothes dragged Becky once more to the ground. This time, she lay still, prostrate in defeat, gasping for breath. She was beaten, the storm lashing her with ridicule and accusations. "Stay down," she heard it say to her. "There's no one to help you!"

Becky was betrayed by her fright and saw only blackness before her. But, then in the darkness, deep down, she saw there the tiniest, smallest flame of courage... and reached for it. In a gesture of rejection of the storm's authority, Becky pulled herself and then Jimmy up, forcing themselves out of the clutches of the gripping mud, and pushed unsteadily forward. Time seemed elusive and only Becky's many pains anchored her to reality, twisting her features as she continued to slip and fall.

Then, with faltering steps, Becky and Jimmy finally staggered into town and headed to the local inn where she hoped they might find information about a coach. Unable to take much money with her, Becky quickly sold what she had for the price of a carriage ride. After that, the money was gone, and she and Jimmy were now forced to use the dangerous roads on foot, eating anything they could could find along the way to keep them alive. Pilfered table scraps meant for a family's dog were often the main fare on their menu. But, Becky didn't care anymore. She was grateful. It had kept her and Jimmy alive. There were already many days where they did not eat at all. Weeks later, when they finally arrived at her family home seeking help and sanctuary, Becky was met with scorn and derision. Considered a scandal in her family's high-society circles, they violently disowned her and firmly closed the door in her bruised face.

The years passed and Jimmy — this was how Becky now addressed him — grew to young boyhood. He was the delight of her life and his smiling face made the long days working to secure enough food for a meagre meal for them all worthwhile. However, Becky knew time was not on their side. Their circumstances continued to fall and the opportunities to earn enough money to eat with a roof over their heads were not plentiful. The Public Workhouse for the Destitute was not far off in their futures and might soon become her and Jimmy's final workplace and residence as it had for so many others whose misfortune it was to have their life's journey end at the gates of that institution.

Overcome by a rush of anxiety and helplessness, Becky quickly covered her eyes with her hand trying desperately not to cry. She feared her persistent small cough would grow serious and that she would have to eventually leave Jimmy to fend for himself. He was already a bit smaller than the other boys his age. And too thin, way too thin, his ribs showing prominently on his small frame when he took off his shirt to wash-up. His prospects would not be good. Yet, Becky believed in the fundamental goodness of life and refused to give up or give in to her desperation, although it would have been so easy to do.

Through these tough years, she had become acutely acquainted with with despair, and recently she had felt the weight of this invisible companion more and more often than she would like to have admitted to herself. But, she also knew despair was just an emotion like any other. It was the *habit* of despair that ultimately condemned a soul. Becky found she could not, would not, walk down that path willingly. She pressed her lips firmly together in renewed determination. Her son, Jimmy, needed her. She would not abandon him. And she believed God *was* watching. If this life was a test, something she believed was true, she would try not to fail Him, at least in that.

Becky looked down at the pitiful amount of money she had earned thus far. Even the small price of two pence on her little handmade sign hadn't brought many 'yes' answers. Still, she had enough now for some food for herself and her little boy — to make it to tomorrow.

"Tomorrow will be a better day," she whispered to herself with hopeful words and hurried to buy some food to take home — where a little boy is waiting.

"A bit of holly for your Christmas?"

The next morning, the Cratchits were up early. Scrooge was to be buried that day and the proper black suits had been laid out. Tim dressed quickly in the cold air of his room, his mind deep in thought of the events that were to take place shortly.

"Tim," his father greeted him as Tim entered the room where he sat drinking a hot cup of tea to ward off the chill that awaited them outside, "come and have something hot to drink."

Tim dutifully obliged and the two sat before the open fire gazing into the flames, each not saying a word, each in a world of his own thoughts.

"Bob! The driver is here," now came the call of Mrs. Cratchit from the next room.

"We'll be right there, Love!" Cratchit called back, standing to finnish the last of his cup before placing it on the mantlepiece. He turned and looked closely at his son. He remembered back to when Tim had been so happy and eager for the future. But, that was now many years ago. He could clearly see that the shadow that had claimed his son was now a deep part of him and would not let him go. Of course, he and Mrs. Cratchit knew why. Now, with the passing of his dear old Mr. Scrooge...

"Tim," Cratchit said softly to remind him that it was time.

"I'll be along, Father, in just a minute," Tim answered wistfully as he continued to stare into the warming fire. Cratchit opened the front door for Mrs. Cratchit without another word being said and the two went outside to wait for Tim in the carriage.

On the way, the sky was gloomy and overcast as the carriage moved along in a steady, but unhurried pace. Mrs. Cratchit had made sure to have the hired carriage pick them up early that morning so they would not have to rush to the cemetery, and her good planning was allowing them a relaxed journey now.

As they travelled across town, Tim's mother and father chatted quietly in respectful tones to pass the time, but Tim was silent, offering not a word the entire journey. Just up ahead, a black iron fence came into view and the driver slowed and parked with the other carriages and coaches already there. Then, as they entered through the high iron gateway on foot, all manner of grave markers could be seen from the large stately monuments of some to the simple tablets inscribed with 'RIP' of many others. And on both sides of the road running through, great trees of oak, bare now in winter, reached out their branches to a sullen sky, looking like great arches in a huge cathedral.

Now, just a short way up the road, a group of people were silently gathered near a coffin and as the Cratchits approached, their presence was acknowledged by a nod of the head from the ladies and a solemn tip of the hat from the gentlemen. Tim and his mother and father moved to a place beneath a sheltering maple and then waited quietly as more people were still arriving.

After everyone was there who wanted to come and say good-bye to old Scrooge, the words 'kind', 'caring', and 'loving man' floated on the cold morning air and drifted in and out of Tim's consciousness as memories of Scrooge came to his mind one after another. Why does God always seem to take away the best of us? Tim thought to himself.

Then, it was over and the crowd moved slowly away, each one giving the coffin a loving and respectful pat as they passed. Finally, only the three Cratchits were left and Tim's mother and father paid their final respects with a silent prayer before moving to where the driver waited with the carriage. Tim was now alone with his friend and his boots crunched on the frozen ground as he walked over to touch Scrooge's headstone. He now noticed that many people had thoughtfully brought holly branches for old Scrooge because they knew that he so loved Christmas.

Tim's own great love for Christmas was in part because of Scrooge's unending all-year-round celebration of the most wonderful day of the year. But, now with Mr. Scrooge gone, what would he do? And what kind of Christmas would this be?

"It won't be any kind of Christmas at all," he answered himself in a voice thick with emotion. "How can it be Christmas without dear old Mr. Scrooge?"

The carriage moved along more quickly on the return journey and in a short time the Cratchits were back home again eating breakfast, one where Tim hardly touched his food. After breakfast, Tim and his father went to work in the old offices of Scrooge & Marley & Cratchit where Tim now worked as a clerk in the same position his father had held for many years.

Snow was beginning to fall as they reached the court where the offices lay and once inside, Cratchit hurriedly started a fire in the grate to take the chill off. With this done, he went about the task of preparing for the day's business. There were ledgers to bring up to date, letters to be written, and orders to be filled. To do all this, Cratchit swiftly darted from one place to another, almost seeming to be everywhere at once.

Meanwhile, Tim climbed onto a high stool at his desk and a candle was lit so he might see the work at hand. Because his corner did not have a window that he might prevail upon, candles illuminated his work space on dark, gloomy days, and this was certainly a two-candle day if ever there was one.

The city clocks now struck the hour nine and Tim looked at the outside door almost as if he expected Scrooge to enter through it as he had every morning at around time. The clocks fell still and the door did not open. Apart from his parents, it was Mr. Scrooge who had made the real difference in his life. Tim remembered back to the cheeriness Mr. Scrooge had brought into every room he entered, his encouragement, and even the countless small kindnesses he had shown him. Many times, Tim had thoughtlessly forgot to even thank him, he now realised. Now, it was too late for all that. Always too late. He lowered his eyes to the work on his desk, but his tears made the figures swim before him.

The silence was again broken as the little bell above the outside door tinkled and a subdued, "Good morning again, gentlemen," came respectfully from the lips of Scrooge's nephew, Fred. He had seen the Cratchits earlier that morning at the cemetery and, together with his own good wife, had chatted briefly with them about how dear a man his Uncle Scrooge had been and how much he would be missed. Fred would now be taking over for his uncle who had worked to the very last day before passing.

"Now, I want you good men to teach me about the business," he offered with his usual modesty, "and I'll try to be as good a pupil as I can be."

All through the day then, that first sad day without Scrooge, many people stopped by for just a moment to say how sorry they were to hear of Scrooge's passing. Meanwhile, Tim stayed purposely at his work refusing to accept the truth that Scrooge was really gone. At five minutes before closing time, Tim put on his hat and coat and said to his father, "I'd like to walk for a little while before I go home, Father. Will that be all right?"

"Of course, Tim," Cratchit answered in a sympathetic tone and understanding on his kind face. "I'll see you at home then."

As Tim opened the door to leave, Fred called out from Scrooge's old office, "Going to do a bit of Christmas shopping, Tim?"

"I don't want to hear anything about Christmas," Tim answered harshly and closed the door firmly behind him.

Cratchit quickly turned to Fred and said how sorry he was that Tim had spoken to him so sharply, but Fred just as quickly allowed that he understood how much Tim missed his uncle and how important Christmas was in their lives.

That night at supper, Tim was quiet and continued to withdraw into himself and almost an hour before his usual bedtime, asked to be excused as it had been a long day. As Tim lay in bed, he thought of his dear Mr. Scrooge and how much he had come to rely on their friendship. Then, as they always did every night, his thoughts went to another. Wetness forced itself from the corners of his eyes. He whispered a name and begged his heart to weep less.

At this same late hour across town in a very poor neighbourhood, Becky and Jimmy watch as their few belongings were roughly thrown out into the snow from their humble one-room lodgings. Their gruff landlord watched as well, and after his two hard-looking hired men had quickly finished their terrible deed, he padlocked the mother and child's front door and hurriedly posted a 'For Rent' sign.

"I told ye when the two of ye moved in, I want me rent on time," the old landlord grumbled as he turned to leave.

"But, I thought... if you would just give us a little more time," Becky pleaded, reaching out her small hand to him apologetically. He scarcely heard her.

"NO! No more time," he barked out his firm answer from angry curled lips. "Yer rent was due yesterday! I don't want to hear any of yer excuses, there can be none!"

But, she could have told him — if he would have listened — that she only had made enough money for a little food so that her boy would not starve and that she would faithfully pay him when she had earned some more, which she fully expected would happen soon, probably tomorrow.

Now, all she could do was watch him disappearing up the street into the blowing snow, pulling his coat collar high to his chin as he passed under a street lamp. She then turned to help her little boy who was now quickly gathering up all their worldly possessions into a very small pile.

"What are we going to do, Mother?" The panic in Jimmy's voice was was apparent. He sat in the snow shivering and hugging his arms in an attempt to ward off the bitter cold. The wind whirled the snow around him now as if trying to take possession of him, to isolate him from any who would try to save the child from its icy grip. Becky quickly snatched Jimmy from the whirlwind that had imprisoned him and then opened her coat and covered the small boy in its folds and dared the might of the storm to claim him from her.

"Everything will be all right, Jimmy!" Becky said trying to sound positive and calming. "We always have, haven't we? I'll tell you what, let's be strong together and sing something. How about *Twinkle, Twinkle Little Star*? That's one of your favourites! Now, let's get our belongings and bring them with us, all right?"

Becky busied herself picking up their one pot that served the dual purpose of cooking and cleaning. They didn't have to worry about a lot of clothes to carry. They were already wearing everything they owned. Soon after, they moved to a nearby abandoned doorway for shelter to wait out the night. Coughing, the brave mother huddled the child close to her and silently prayed for a miracle to save them.

Lost to sight in the snowy storm, the eerie sounds of voices singing an old English nursery rhyme drifted in and out on the edges of the howling wind.

Praying for a Miracle

STAVE 2

The Return

The last few days just before Christmas at Scrooge & Marley & Cratchit were busy days, too busy for Cratchit or Fred to have time to notice that Tim was growing more and more sad and withdrawn with each day that passed. His grieving kept on coming and just doing what was required was exhausting. He went through the motions of getting up in the morning, going to work, and coming home again, but mostly because he couldn't think of anything else he could do. His life had become an act of irrelevance.

The yuletide was in full bloom now with the poulterer's shop doing a brisk business in close running with the grocer's and the fruiterer's and the baker's shops. But, even with all of this merriment going on and all of the Yuletide music, all of the season's greetings and good cheer being wished with "Merry Christmas!" from everyone to everyone, it meant nothing to Tim, not a single thing.

Finally, it was the day of Christmas Eve and Tim sat in his cell-like corner lighted by a single candle copying letters. The weather beyond the frosted front windows was biting cold and miserable and the fog was so thick it almost seemed to invade the office itself. Horses going by were better recognised for their sound than the sight of them. But now, they eerily clip-clopped past on the narrow court in front like ghostly phantoms floating in some kind of fantasy of the mind.

The city clocks struck four just as Fred came bounding into the office with a cheery, "Merry Christmas to all, gentlemen, and I do mean all!"

"Happy Christmas yourself, Fred!" Cratchit returned, joining in the same high spirits and good feelings of the season that Fred had displayed. Then, silence hung without any response from Tim who continued to his work.

The offices of Scrooge & Marley & Cratchit — Fred asked that the name not be changed to include him — closed at four-thirty on Christmas Eve, but though it was now only ten past, Fred clapped his hands together and proposed, "Why don't we call it a day, gentlemen? It'll be my treat to a Christmas bowl of smoking bishop at London Tavern to honour in the season. It would please me greatly!"

"I have a little more work to do, I'm afraid," Tim replied politely, rejecting the offer. "But, thank you kindly, anyway."

Cratchit looked at Fred with an expression of resignation as Tim returned to his work and, with a shrug of his shoulders, put on his coat and hat to leave. They both knew that it was useless to pursue him with their good humour the way he felt and the two withdrew as gracefully as they could.

"I'll see you later on then, Tim ," Cratchit said as he opened the door for Fred. Tim nodded 'yes' to his father and the two men left with the little bell above the outside door seeming to tinkle a little longer than usual.

As Tim continued to work on to finish the last of the letters to be copied, Christmas music from the carollers outside in the street drifted into the offices with a haunting sound: *"Everything that I see, is saying to me, Christmas time is getting near..."*

BONG! went the first solemn toll of the bell from the ancient tower of the church, and then dragged on slowly toward its fifth number as if the whole world was waiting for the clock's permission to continue on, but only after the final bell had been struck.

Now, it was about this time of day that Scrooge had always called to Tim from his office doorway, "Tim,'bout that time." This meant closing time, time to put the books away.

Suddenly, through the distorted music seeping in at every crack, crevice, and keyhole, came a voice echoing as if down a long empty hallway: "*Tiiiiiimm...*"

Tim looked up from his work with startled surprise and, though he knew there was not a soul in the place but himself, answered, "Yes?" He quickly cast a wary eye toward the doorway where Scrooge had always stood at closing time and then around the room as if expecting to see someone there. No, no one there, but the place looked different somehow, *brighter.* Shaking his head in the negative and dismissing it now as just his imagination, the place dimmed and returned to the darkness of before.

Finally, he finished the last letter, climbed down from his high perch, and started to blow out the candle. But before he could, the voice once again came hollow through the twisted music just beyond the frosted front windows: "*Tiiiiiimm...*"

Tim STOPPED and listened intently as he extended the candle out as far as his arm could reach and examined the room carefully. Again, nothing there.

"Tiiiiiimm..."

Carrying the flame with him now, he crossed the offices to the coat pegs at the front door and placed his desk candle with the lighted one already there. Then, after putting on his coat and scarf and taking one last enquiring look around, he extinguished both candles in one blow and quickly vacated the premises.

Outside, the courtyard was ablaze with festive candles lighting every shop window, and everywhere green sprigs of Christmas holly and red berries were present, trimmed out in their holiday finest with red bows added for good measure. And the grocers, the poulterers, the bakers, and sweet makers, one and all were doing a business as never before.

With all of this activity going on, all of the carollers singing songs of the season and all the little bands playing and the sellers selling and the buyers buying looked and sounded like a beautiful scene from one of the great operas.

As Tim went along his melancholy way through the crowded streets of merrymakers and last-minute shoppers, his thoughts turned to other Christmas Eves and how wonderful they had been when Mr. Scrooge was there and they were together.

"Happy Christmas, Tim!" came a warm greeting shouted his way from the poulterer's shop as he passed. Tim winced at the words, suddenly feeling indignant at their meaning, and troubled emotions darkened his features. He answered the salutation with a wave of his hand and continued on without speaking. Up ahead now, a little girl was running from a little boy and both were laughing heartily after the girl had snatched the boy's hat from his head and promised to never give it back.

Sadly, Tim thought how much she reminded him of Becky. With renewed bitterness, Tim's thoughts once more turned to his lost love. After Becky had been taken from him, Tim had searched and searched years for her without success. Eventually, he had to accept that she was forever lost from his life. All he knew was that he wasn't there when she needed him the most. She was his soul mate. And he had failed her. Failed her. He had grown to hate the disappointment he had become in his own eyes. For Tim, there really wasn't any other way to look at it. How do you live with something like that? "You don't," Tim answered aloud. He didn't even get to say good-bye.

Through the following years, Tim had desperately tried to forget the pain of his failure, to forget about her, to move on with his life. He found he couldn't do it. He had loved her too much, too deeply, loved her still and knew he would never be free of it.

> *Except for the times I breathe in,*
> *I think of you only when I breathe out...*

Tim had made great efforts over the years to look and sound normal to his family and friends, to smile and laugh on cue when the correct occasion called for it. But inside, he had become broken. And now recently, he had begun to notice perplexed looks on people's faces, suspicious glances that his answers were a bit off, that something wasn't quite right with him. But, none of this seemed to matter much to Tim anymore. Nothing mattered, really. He was tired. Very tired. Caring was now a luxury that was beyond him. Each day he felt there was less of himself to hold onto as if slowly fading away from this world. And he was alright with that. If he could have stopped his own heart, he would have gladly.

Tim's unfocused eyes now stared down at the ground. He had never understood the reasons *why* their marriage had been forbidden or in her belief that there was a reason and to accept God's will. *God's will.* His anger at God had started only as a small ember, but had continued to grow through the years. Now, his doubts about God's helpfulness had become a certainty. Not only in his own life, but in anyone else's as well. Tim saw broken lives and poverty and misery everywhere. Where was God in these people's lives? At least, Mr. Scrooge had been a light in a darkening world.

Tim stopped by Cornhill on his way home to watch the boys and girls slide, and he remembered how proud he had been when he was little and Mr. Scrooge had watched him slide. A beggar came toward him now and offered his outstretched cap to receive anything that Tim might want to give him in his hour of need. Tim automatically reached into his pocket for some coins just as he'd always done because of Scrooge's often taught, "Share what you have, and you share what you are." He started to pull the coins from his pocket then stopped, gripped the money tightly, and evading the man's eyes, stiffly walked on.

Even the music of the Christmas season that he had loved so much couldn't touch his heart growing colder and harder with each beat. He passed the stores where he and Becky had often spent hours and hours window shopping, excitedly planning for what they would want and need in their lives together. But it was never to be. The memory made him ache for her. Angrily, Tim trudged on through the bustling and crowded streets, his eyes hot with distress. Suddenly, he became aware of a little girl standing in front of him and blocking his path, saying something, and offering a small shiny object up to him. As he tried to make some sense of her words, she placed a small piece of metal in his hand.

"I found it," she said. "And you can have it." She then left in a hurry, running up the street before Tim could refuse, and he now stood staring down at a tiny cross.

With that one small act, he was undone and the weight of his disappointments came crashing down. Clutching the cross so hard that his hand began to bleed, Tim shook a defiant fist and raged at the silent heavens.

"Why! Why! Why!" Tim's injured soul screamed over and over again to an indifferent sky. Then, with nothing more to say, Tim fell hard to his knees as anguish flared across his face. "Oh, Becky, my love... dear old Mr. Scrooge, my good friend..." His losses felt as poignant as a verdict and his desolate soul wanted to weep.

And then he was weeping. Hunched over as if he were trying to limit the exposure of his failures, Tim continued to kneel in the snow for a long time, his thoughts turned inward to himself as he cradled his hurt. Then, with a finality that comes only with loss, Tim crushed the cross in a tightening fist and coldly whispered to himself, "I don't need anyone anymore." Weak from his exertion, Tim slowly struggled to his feet and straightened up. He felt strangely detached as if his caring were being poured onto the ground like a pitcher of water. Emptying. Empty. Gone. For anything or anyone. After a few more moments of thought, he raised his swollen eyes to look out upon the Christmas scene as his hand swung down to his side, and then, after considering it all, he released the gift to fall into the snow.

It was a quarter past nine when Tim finally arrived home and when he opened the door, his mother stopped helping his father trim the Christmas tree and hurried to set a place for him at the table. She had kept his supper warm so it would be every bit as good as it would have been had he been there at his usual time of half past five. When he had finished eating, Tim settled into a comfortable chair by the fire and listened to his father tell stories of Christmases he had known as a young boy. Quite animated and enthusiastic, Cratchit spun his tales of olde and the good mood of Christmas captured the house in its spell, assisted by candlelight from every branch of the Yule tree. Adding even more to the warm Cratchit family scene was the smell of Christmas tree mingled with mince pies baking and chestnuts roasting and plum pudding waiting its turn. *Ding!* went the mantlepiece clock.

"Quarter past, my dear," Cratchit said and rose from his chair near the fire and stretched to convey his intention. Mrs. Cratchit immediately began blowing out the candles on the tree in preparation for bed, but Tim continued to sit, staring into the fire.

After the house was made snug for the night and everything put away, Cratchit turned to Tim with a consoling voice and said, "Good night, Tim. See you in the morning, son," as he and Mrs. Cratchit started up the stairs to their bed.

"Good night, Father. Good night, Mother. Sleep well," Tim answered without turning in their direction, still staring into the fire.

The house grew quiet now. Only an occasional crack from the burning logs broke the silence. Then, *Ding! Ding! Ding!* the mantlepiece clock struck out its final warning before the midnight hour, and Tim took the candle and went upstairs to his bed.

He quickly put on his nightshirt and cap because, even though his bedroom was directly above the room with the fireplace, it still was cold. At night when the fire downstairs had reduced itself to just a memory, the flannel in his bed clothes and the warm down of his goose-feather filled mattress and pillow were welcome companions. Pulling back the covers now with purpose, Tim didn't waste any time getting into bed for this night he was especially tired and eager to abandon himself to the hollowness of his dreams. Soon, he was asleep and the night began to tick away.

STAVE 3

The Ghost

Now, the bell in the church belfry struck out its methodic infor-
mative: Nine, Ten, Eleven, Twelve — Midnight! Even before the
last toll had faded away, the ominous voice Tim had heard in the offices the afternoon before at his desk was again calling out his name:
"Tiiiiiimm…"

Startled into awakening, Tim now raised himself halfway up onto
one elbow and stared at the doorway into the hall wence the voice had
seemed to come.

"Who is it? Who is it?" Tim blurted out in quick succession, trying
to pierce the blurriness of his sleepy eyes and the sparsely lighted room.
Then, slowly a figure became apparent standing in the doorway of his
room.

"WHO is it?" Tim pleaded again, now in a voice of sheer panic.

"It is I, Tim… Ebenezer."

Tim's mouth actually dropped open as he recoiled in shock and
panic against the headboard of his bed. After a few moments, he was
able to recover enough to exclaim, "Mr. Scrooge!"

"Yes, Tim, it is I."

"But, how can it be?" Tim questioned now in total disbelief, still plastered against his headboard. The ghost became illuminated now like an oil lamp being turned up slowly by an unseen hand, and Tim could plainly see that it surely looked like Mr. Scrooge. Still, he kept his iron grip on his bedpost as he watched the ghost come nearer and nearer, right to the foot of his bed! His first thought was to pull his feet up away from the end of the bed where the ghost stood peering down at him through vacant eyes, but his body was so rigid from fright it wouldn't cooperate.

Scrooge's Ghost

But, it was Scrooge, all right, no doubt about it. None whatsoever. The same long white hair, the same mutton chop sideburns down his face, the same chiselled nose. There was no mistaking him, it was Scrooge! He was almost transparent and still wearing the same cap and night-shirt he had been wearing when he passed away in his sleep and Tim could easily see the candle behind him that was kept lit at night in the hallway right through his body. Adding much to the eeriness of the fore-boding scene was the unearthly glow emanating from the ghost that not only illuminated the ghost, but also himself and his bed and, to some degree, the room itself.

Though the apparition was close enough to touch — if he had wanted to, which he did not at the moment — Tim began to feel less fear now at this ghostly encounter because he had loved Scrooge so much.

"You may wonder why I'm here," Scrooge's ghost asked with a concerned tone and a frown on his ashen face.

"The thought had occurred to me, sir," Tim answered perplexed and sat up a little taller in bed.

"Sometimes, Tim, on very special occasions, we are allowed to return to earth if our presence here is needed. We are allowed to endeavour to assist those who are having a problem and need our help."

"Are there those here, then, who are having a problem and need your help, Mr. Scrooge?"

"Yes, Tim, I think there are," the ghost answered emphatically.

"But, why do you come to see me?" Tim questioned pointedly.

"I need you to help me, Tim, to help three people," the ghost explained. "I would like you to come with me now to help me with this problem."

"Now? But, Mr. Scrooge! It's night time and cold out there! Can't it wait until tomorrow?"

"These people need our help now, Tim. Tomorrow is a place where many things never get done."

"Well, yes then, of course, Mr. Scrooge, if you feel it is that important," Tim replied. "Just wait until I put my clothes and coat on."

"You won't need to do that, Tim," the ghost said gently. "Just touch my sleeve and you will not be cold this winter's night nor seen by anyone but me."

Tim did as Scrooge's ghost instructed and the two of them passed right through the outside wall of his upstairs bedroom and reappeared on a snowy street in Camden Town, a part of the city for those with modest means.

The place seemed familiar to Tim and he couldn't help saying to the ghost, "Mr. Scrooge, it seems I've been here before, a long time ago," and as he said this, a little boy came out of a door nearby. He looked to be poor and was tiny, thin, and frail and walked with a small crutch to help him because of his withered legs.

Tim watched closely as the little boy passed them and then with excited surprise exclaimed, "That's me, Mr. Scrooge, me, when I was a little boy!"

"Yes, Tim," the ghost said knowingly. "You as you were fourteen Christmases ago."

As Tim and the ghost watched, the little boy stood and waited for his father to come out of the house, whilst nearby, some boys were throwing snowballs at one another and were laughing and shouting good-natured taunts in the game. The crippled little boy could only watch the playful frolicking and romping in the snow with unwavering interest and a sad look of longing.

"Do you remember this, Tim?" the ghost asked gently. Without taking his eyes from the small, lame boy, Tim answered, "I remember," and in that brief instant realised how much he had forgotten to be thankful for.

"Touch my sleeve once again, Tim," Scrooge's ghost urged and again Tim obeyed. They reappeared in a court in the middle of the city and fog obscured their view, but as they crossed the courtyard a sign could now be read: Scrooge & Marley.

"I know where we are now!" Tim said with certainty. "This is your office before Father became your partner a long time ago."

"Yes, Tim. Let's go in and see how it was then before your father's promotion." They passed on through the outside wall of the offices and now stood in the ill-lighted office of Ebenezer Scrooge... and with Scrooge at his desk. The door of Scrooge's office was open with a full view of the much colder outer office where his devoted clerk, Bob

Cratchit now laboured in his tiny cell-like desk space. Scrooge purposely kept his door open so he could spy on Cratchit's every move, and Cratchit could feel the heat from his constant observation. It was about the only warmth he ever got in that cold place, poor fellow.

Scrooge kept the coal box for both fires just inside the door of his room and guarded it like a cashbox full of gold, not to be spent. But, now at this defining moment of misery, Cratchit had suffered the cold for about as long as he thought he could take, the warmth from the small fire that had resided in his grate having escaped the premises some time ago. Emboldened now to action and determined, he moved stealthily — on his hands and knees, shovel in hand — toward the hoarded prize just inches away. Scrooge pretended not to notice the cat-like Cratchit, waiting until his shivering clerk had reached for a lump of the black gold, then with practised precision timing, he snapped, "Cratchit! Mr. Cratchit!"

"Sir?" cringed the clerk like a whimpering dog. "My fire has all but gone cold. There's not a bit of heat left in it."

He didn't get any further with his sad story because Scrooge intoned condescendingly, "Mr. Cratchit, your duties here do not include wasting our coal. Please be good enough to return to your work or I shall deduce from your lack of industry that we are destined to part."

"Yes, Mr. Scrooge," Cratchit replied obediently and quickly got his scarf to put around his neck to ward off the chill, leaving still his other important parts from his neck up and his neck down to fend for themselves.

"A Merry Christmas, Uncle, God save you!" came the joyous proclamation of Scrooge's nephew, Fred, as he entered the establishment now.

"Bah!" said old Scrooge. "Humbug!"

Old Scrooge

"Christmas a humbug, Uncle?" the nephew questioned. "You don't mean that, I am sure."

"I do," said Scrooge. "Merry Christmas!" he mimicked. "What right have you to be merry? What reason have you to be merry? You're poor enough."

"Come then, what right have you to be dismal? What reason have you to be morose?" the nephew returned in his usual good-natured way, "You're rich enough."

Tim now turned to Scrooge's ghost in amazement. "Did you say those things, Mr. Scrooge?"

"Yes, Tim," the ghost answered sadly. "I'm sorry to say I did." Tim and Scrooge's ghost now turned back toward Scrooge just as two portly gentlemen approached him jovially.

"Scrooge and Marley's, I believe?" said the portlier of the two referring to his list. "Have I the pleasure of addressing Mr. Scrooge or Mr. Marley?" he enquired graciously, punctuating his warm delivery with a little jut of his prodigious belly.

Scrooge informed them that his partner had passed on seven years ago this very night and waited impatiently for their reason for being there.

"At this festive season of the year, Mr. Scrooge," the man began with pen at the ready, "it is more than usually desirable that we should make some slight provision for the poor and destitute who suffer greatly at the present time. Many thousands are in want of common necessaries, hundreds of thousands are in need of common comforts, sir."

"Are there no prisons?" Scrooge quickly enquired. "And the union workhouses? Are they still in operation?" he continued excitedly, sounding alarmed and fearful of their unfortunate demise.

"They are still," returned the gentleman remorsefully. "I wish I could say they were not."

Again, Tim turned to Scrooge's ghost enquiringly.

"Yes, Tim, it's all true," the ghost acknowledged sadly before Tim could ask the hurtful question. "That's how it was then," he added with his head bowed. His face held the look of too many memories. Turning back now to Scrooge and the gracious solicitors still ripe with conviviality despite Scrooge's unsympathetic attitude, Tim and Scrooge's ghost listened as the man with the pen and notebook enquired hopefully.

"What shall I put you down for?"

"Nothing!" replied Scrooge.

"You wish to be anonymous?" The man's face brightened.

"I wish to be left alone," Scrooge dashed his hopes. "Since you ask me what I wish, gentlemen, that is my answer. I don't make merry myself at Christmas and I can't afford to make idle people merry. I help to support the establishments I have mentioned — they cost enough, and those who are badly off must go there ."

"Many can't go there," replied the solicitor and then added sadly, "and many would rather die!"

"Well, if they would rather die," returned Scrooge with lofty indifference, "they had better do it and decrease the surplus population."

"Oh, please... let's leave here. Please!" Tim urgently pleaded to Scrooge's ghost, obviously troubled and saddened by how hard and uncompassionate Scrooge had been to his fellow man, and at Christmas of all times. Tim was truly shocked to see a terrible side of a man he thought he knew.

"Touch my sleeve, Tim," Scrooge's ghost now commanded like a schoolmaster about to teach an important lesson, and Tim did, and instantly they were in a bedchamber. On the bed Tim could see Scrooge grasping at his bedpost and heard him mumbling, "I will honour Christmas in my heart and try to keep it all the year. I will live in the past, the present, and the future. The spirits of all three shall strive within me."

Instantly, upon Scrooge's promise of reformation, church bells began ringing here, there, everywhere, preventing Scrooge from uttering any further discourse. And like a little child, he ran to the window, flung it open, and put out his head.

As Tim and Scrooge's ghost watched and listened, Scrooge called down to a boy dressed in Sunday clothes on the street below.

"What's today?"

"Eh?" replied the boy, obviously quick and right on top of his game.

"What's today, my fine fellow!" Scrooge tried again.

"Today?" replied the boy. "Why, Christmas Day."

"It's Christmas Day!" Scrooge repeated to himself with delight. "I haven't missed it," he gushed joyfully. "Hallo, my fine fellow!" he bellowed at the boy.

"Hallo!" the boy bellowed right back.

"Do you know the poulterer's in the next street, but one at the corner?" called Scrooge.

"I should hope I did," replied the lad.

"An intelligent boy," said Scrooge to himself, "A remarkable boy," he went on glowingly. "Do you know whether they've sold the prize turkey that was hanging up there? Not the little prize turkey, the big one?" (He raised his flattened hand horizontally to just under his chin to indicate the bird's awesome proportions).

"What, the one as big as me?" returned the boy. "It's hanging there now."

"It is? Go and buy it then!" Scrooge shouted waving his finger toward the direction of the poulterer's shop.

"Walk-er!" exclaimed the boy (meaning: Right, Gov'nor. I'll catch the next cab).

"No, no," said Scrooge, "I am in earnest. Go and buy it and tell them to bring it here that I may give them the directions where to take it. Come back with the man and I'll give you a shilling. Come back with him in less than five minutes and I'll give you half a crown!" The boy was gone in the blink of an eye and Scrooge danced again in anticipation of the boy's return with the poulterer.

"I'll send it to Bob Cratchit!" bubbled Scrooge to himself with delighted glee. "He shan't know who sends it."

Tim now turned to Scrooge's ghost with a furrowed brow of puzzlement and stammered, "B-but, I thought... back in those days you were—"

"Mean? Selfish? Stingy?" the ghost finished Tim's question.

"Well, yes," Tim answered hesitantly, "all of those things, I dare say. I don't quite understand, Mr. Scrooge."

"That was my former self, Tim, the way I was. Then, I changed just as we all can change and be better for it. I learned that money was not my main business in this life, that money has no worth of its own. Its good is derived from what it can do to help other people, Tim. People are *everything*! Remember that, Tim. Remember it always."

And with that, the ghost of Ebenezer Scrooge faded slowly away and Tim was back in his own room again, in his own bed, and was fast asleep.

STAVE 4

The Last Haunting

N ow, after what only seemed like a short time, the church bell was again striking out its numbers: Nine, Ten, Eleven, Twelve — Midnight! Then, once again came the soul-wrenching voice of the ghost of Ebenezer Scrooge: *"Tiiiiiimm..."*

"Yes?" Tim answered sleepily, struggling to open his eyes by raising his eyebrows. Succeeding, he could see Scrooge's ghost as he had been before standing at the foot of his bed.

"I still need you, Tim," he half whispered, "to help me to help those three people."

Tim was out of bed without another word, and when the ghost offered his sleeve, Tim touched it and they were off again. This time they flew over the city with snow-covered rooftops laid out white below them. Then, once more they were standing on a cold London street, peering through an old iron gate so obscured by fog and darkness that it completely hid the dreary pile of a building lying just beyond.

As Tim strained to see through the unrelenting fog and frost that hung like an icy shroud about the old gateway, everything became light as if the dawn had come up in just a moment.

Before Tim could say a word, for surely he knew where they were now, the front door of the old building opened and out came Scrooge in a flurry. He quickly closed the door behind him and bounded nimbly to the gate in the street. Then, stopping for just a moment as he looked around appraising the new day with obvious pleasure, he observed appreciatively — as if seeing it for the first time — "What a wonderful morning!"

Love for humanity and a delight for living beamed from his smiling face as he strolled along the street greeting everyone with "Merry Christmas!" and tipping his hat to all he met along the way. And when coming upon the gracious solicitors from the preceding day, whom he had rejected for a donation for the needy, he made generous amends by giving a huge sum for the poor and would not let them accept a farthing less, confessing, "A great many back payments are included in it, I assure you."

Tim had not taken his hand from the ghost's sleeve and now they were instantly transported to another place where Scrooge was just coming to a large old house. Above the door a sign read 'Orphanage' and as Tim and Scrooge's ghost moved closer, they could see a housekeeper out the back spanking the carpets with her broom as if it were their punishment for being dirty.

"Merry Christmas, dear heart!" Scrooge called to the woman, smiling so broadly that his grin actually seemed to start from beneath the great mutton chop sideburns next to his ears.

"Oh, Mr. Scrooge! Merry Christmas to you and yours too, I'm sure!" declared the housekeeper with delight at seeing him. "Please, go right in! The door is open for you."

Scrooge removed his hat and stamped his feet on the porch to remove the snow with such rhythm that he seemed to be doing a dance, and if you would have put a tune to it, it would have been a lively song of joy to be sure.

Inside, Tim and Scrooge's ghost watched as word spread that, "Mr. Scrooge is here!"

At this news, bedlam reigned in the large front hallway as cascades of boys and girls poured down the winding staircase like a waterfall of chattering little faces. Such "oohing" and "aahing" at the wonder of their expectations never was heard in that hallway before as Scrooge stood with his outstretched arms to receive them. In moments, he was completely engulfed in little people hugging and showering him with their loving adulation.

Scrooge tried his best to acknowledge every hand thrust in his direction with a "Merry Christmas!" and when the little hand had a pleading voice to go with it that called, "Mr. S-c-r-o-o-g-e," he quickly rewarded the call with a git from the big red bag he had requested the toy shop deliver earlier that morning.

Tim now turned to Scrooge's ghost with great admiration at the warm, inspiring sight he was witnessing and said, "They all love you so much — I mean, him so much," he corrected himself.

"Yes, Tim, I believe they did," the ghost replied brightly. "And he loved every one of them too just as much, and maybe even more."

"Oh dear, Mr. Scrooge," Tim began humbly as if a great revelation were taking place, "it occurs to me only now, at this very moment, that I missed something terribly important about you when you were here, something that I might have learned from you had I thought to look beyond myself. I can see now that even with all the time you found for me to help me in my life, that you were doing more, infinitely more, than just helping me. I wonder now that you ever found the time to do the good things you did like caring after these poor little orphan children. But, I guess you did for you must have seen these little ones often, they know you so well."

"When something is important to you, Tim, as God gives you the strength, you make the time for it. And whilst it is true that one person cannot cure the troubles of the whole world, they can make things better in their own little corner of it and then pass the spirit of giving on to those who will follow. Do you understand these things I'm telling you, Tim?"

Tim did not reply immediately. With hands clasped in front of him, Scrooge's ghost stood silent and waited patiently for Tim to come to terms with his personal crisis.

Finally, Tim replied in a soft voice that cracked with emotion. "Yes, Mr. Scrooge. I am starting to understand. But, I fear I don't have that strength anymore. I have been... very angry. Angry at God. Devastated at the way things turned out for me, wondering where God was when things went wrong. Hadn't I been a good person? Why me?" Turning to look out a window, Tim continued with a husky emptiness in his voice. "I feel so abandoned... and alone. I have lost so very much" — Tim now clenched his eyes shut — "that was dear to me. I prayed, and prayed, and prayed," Tim continued, punctuating his words in an angry rhythm.

"I ask you, where did any of it get me? God did *not* answer me. God was silent. Now... even you're gone as well. Look — I've tried to work on my faith, but I have reached the end. I'm just existing from one long day to the next. I'm just waiting for my time to end here. I failed. Failed." Tim's voice had begun to take on a hysterical and dangerous edge as he spoke at a furious pace, now more to himself than to Scrooge's ghost. "I don't even know why I'm here now. I don't deserve to be here anymore. I can never redeem myself. Never."

Tim stopped speaking for a moment, then continued in a voice riven with grief. "I just want to be dead. Need to be dead. There is nothing here for me anymore. It's all so meaningless now. I live such a useless life..." Tim then turned to look at Scrooge's ghost. "Don't you understand?" Tim screamed, "I don't want to be here anymore!" Turning his back on Scrooge's ghost now to look out the window once more, he added quietly, "I just want the pain to end. Oh, please... just let there be an end."

"I know you have been angry, Tim," Scrooge replied in a sympathetic voice. "Even more, you have been sorely hurt, and that affected your faith in Him. But, you were never alone. Even when you felt Him farthest from you, that was when He was closest to you. Our circumstances do change, but His truths never do.

"Tim, listen to me. Try to understand. Real faith isn't about the belief that He will fix everything when things go wrong because you have been a good person. That isn't how it works. True faith is trusting Him even when you don't understand the *why* of things that happen to good people. It is one of the hardest things we are asked to do. Perhaps, the hardest. Our faith is especially tested at those times that are the bleakest in our lives and nothing seems to makes sense. But in this, we are not choiceless, and we are not alone.

"You can choose to trust Him even when you don't understand, and choose to be content because you trust Him with your life in His hands. God has a plan for you, for all people, for He has proclaimed to us, "Be still, and know that I am GOD.""

"Be content?"

"Yes."

"God has a plan for me?" Tim questioned bitterly.

"Yes."

"And I am supposed to believe in Him even when my life is in shambles?"

"Yes, Tim. An untested faith is no faith at all. God said there would be storms in our lives, but to hold true. Many, many fail and fall away from God, not unlike yourself. Liken your faith as to a ship at sea. As a ship does not move in calm waters, so your faith languishes also. But, a faith that holds true over life's trials and sorrows is very, very precious to God."

Tim did not say anything for a while. "But, Mr. Scrooge, why does God allow such misery in the world, such hatred, and evil, and indifference?"

"Is not hatred a choice?" Scrooge's ghost replied, "Or being evil a choice? Isn't our indifference to the suffering of others a choice? God gave us the power of choice. And it's the choices we make that determine our lives and affects the lives of those around us. Wherefore, do we not all help shape the world in which we live?

"But, let me answer you even more directly: whilst God is not the source of our problems here on earth, I do believe He allows these problems to teach us something important we need to learn. I believe that God, at times, allows the difficulties in people's lives to challenge their faith to grow. It prepares us for an even higher level of faith and connection that is ever closer to His promises and purifies and strengthens us for His purposes. And as our increasing difficulties are matched by an increasing faith, we are rewarded with a new level of God's grace. Only in the storm do you see God's glory in its fullest.

"So, if our lives are truly in His hands, then begin to rely on Him and let God fight your battles. Press on and shake off your weariness and despair and stop complaining. For you do not see what He sees or know what He knows. Submit to His will and be content, no matter what has befallen you or your circumstances. Do *not* give up and rely on Him for it is written: 'Trust in the Lord and lean not on your own understanding'".

"But, what of my prayers? I needed God to help me... and God didn't," Tim persisted.

"God responds to *faith*, Tim, not *needs*. Did you pray for a something or for Him to be a presence and the strength in your life?"

Chastened, Tim's pained visage looked down at the floor as if he would be able to find there a denial to the ghost's words. But, he could not. He had never given God that kind of fidelity.

Now, feeling both foolish and unworthy, Tim replied in a sober whisper, "I am beginning to understand a little now, Mr. Scrooge. Finally.

"But, tell me then, if you will, if I have failed in my faith, why does He even care?"

The eyes of the ghost bore into him with a special intensity and would not release him. But, with a gentleness in his voice that was as surprising as an act of charity, Scrooge's ghost answered Tim's question. "Because, He is *mercy* itself. He understands anguish and despair. He understands. And because He understands, I, myself, was given a second chance." Scrooge's ghost looked down with deep humility and then back up to look at Tim and smiled. "And... am I not with you now?"

Respectfully, Tim asked one more question. "But, Mr. Scrooge, there are so many people with problems like mine or maybe even worse. Who's going to help them?"

"I helped you and your family, didn't I?" the ghost replied as he offered Tim his sleeve to touch.

Tim quickly looked up, his eyes wide in surprise. But, before he could say anything, they were again mysteriously transported to another place — this time to an old red-brick building on the edge of the city.

"Where are we now, Mr. Scrooge?" Tim asked with a puzzled tone in his voice.

"This is a place where people go, Tim, when they haven't the means to stay anywhere else. "The poorhouse," he added then as if it was breaking his heart to say the words.

"What do people do here?" Tim questioned with concern showing in his voice.

"Hope, Tim. Just hope. Hope that someone will care enough to help them."

Now, Scrooge's ghost and Tim moved closer and listened in as Scrooge spoke with those in charge.

"Is everyone getting enough to eat now and have everything they need?" Scrooge asked excitedly with his hands clasped in front of him in a pose that made him look as if he were praying.

"Oh yes, Mr. Scrooge. Thanks be to you," praised the man in charge.

"May I see them for a few minutes?" Scrooge pleaded. "It's Christmas, you know."

"Yes, Mr. Scrooge, I know, and of course you can," replied the man warmly, showing his admiration for the benevolent benefactor. As soon as the residents heard that Ebenezer was there, Scrooge was engulfed in a sea of faces, though this time, quite a bit older than the ones from before, yet the same — so glad to see him.

"Ebenezer! Ebenezer!" they called to him as they reached for his outstretched hand and crowded in around him so tightly that one could hardly move. He had to shake every hand or pat every shoulder and hug everyone in a wheelchair who was there. Nothing less would have ever satisfied old Scrooge, nor could he be content until he had said "Merry Christmas!" to every smiling face in that happy, happy group of people who just wanted to be with him.

As Scrooge moved joyfully through his throng of good friends, Scrooge's ghost turned to Tim who was watching the heart-warming scene with rapt attention and said, "We must be going now, Tim, my time here grows short."

"These people are so wonderful, Mr. Scrooge," Tim replied to the ghost with warm amazement in his voice, "I hate to leave."

But, Scrooge's ghost gently insisted by offering his sleeve and when Tim touched it, they were whisked to a part of the city that Tim definitely didn't recognise. It was a poor, rundown part of town, even poorer than where he had spent his own early childhood. The houses were little more than dirty patched up shacks, and all kinds of odds and ends materials were in use to try to stave off winter's deadly cold. The walls were dark from the soot of countless years, and grimy windows, many with broken panes mended with boards and rags, were much in evidence. A rivulet of foul water trickled down the centre of the dank alley where they stood and gave the place the stench of decay.

"Where is this, Mr. Scrooge?" Tim asked bewilderedly, wrinkling his nose at the smell and looking up and down the street for a clue to the mystery. But, before the ghost could answer, a door opened on the other side of the street and a little boy with a scarf as long as himself (longer for it was touching the ground) came running out.

"Come on, Mother!" urged the boy jumping up and down with childish expectation. "Pleeeease!"

Out of the door now came a pretty young lady with a broken wicker basket that was held together with string and a dirty ribbon that at one time in its past might have been a bright yellow. She looked to be about Tim's age, and Tim watched with a special interest as the mother put her basket down and retied the little boy's long scarf so it wouldn't drag the ground. As he watched, Tim couldn't help noticing the mother's oft mended, threadbare coat that hung loosely on her gaunt frame, or the little boy's patched coat that was hardly more than tatters.

"Strange, Mr. Scrooge," Tim said softly with his voice breaking in pity, "it seems... I may know her..." he continued, straining to get a better look at the face of the woman who was partially turned away from him.

"Really!" said the ghost with feigned surprise and a sideward glance that Tim didn't notice because his eyes were preoccupied elsewhere.

"Oh, my Lord!" Tim exclaimed taken by complete surprise as she finally turned towards him. "It's Becky!"

In a rush of conflicting emotions, Tim was shocked by the changes in her physical condition and circumstance, but his heart also pounded with so much excitement and delight at seeing her again that he felt it might burst. "I went to school with her!" he breathlessly poured out his story to Scrooge's ghost. "We were… very good friends." Tim had never revealed to Scrooge or to his family how deep his feelings for Becky were having been too shy to express them. Nor did Tim reveal to his parents or old Scrooge that he had asked Becky to marry him, or how she was torn from his life as a result of his love for her. "Becky!"

Without any thought, Tim automatically started toward Becky, the need to be with her too strong for him to control. But, Scrooge's ghost restrained him.

"No, Tim. They cannot see you or hear you."

"Is she going to meet her husband?" Tim asked expecting a 'yes'.

"No. She doesn't have a husband," the ghost replied sombrely.

"Doesn't have a husband!" Tim repeated with his voice rising with surprise and concern.

"He's gone, Tim," the ghost answered in a way that seemed to make further explanation unnecessary. "Touch my sleeve, Tim, one more time," Scrooge's ghost said softly offering his arm, and Tim gently laid his hand on it almost out of habit now as he was still staring at Becky and the little boy and thinking about all the things he'd just seen and heard.

They quickly reappeared on a snowy London street corner where Christmas trees were being sold and bargained for and a ruddy-faced man in a great coat that was but an inch or two above his shoes was just completing a sale. Becky and her little boy were waiting their turn to be helped and the boy was dutifully going from tree to tree inspecting each one for his mother.

"Can I'elp you, ma'am?" intoned the tree seller with the smile of a merchant.

"Yes, we would like to know... that is... what your Christmas trees cost... for the small ones?" she added quickly to make clear she wanted a tree that wasn't too expensive.

"'alf a crown," replied the seller in a voice and attitude that made one believe that he thought he was giving them away at that price and would probably go broke at any moment because of his generosity.

"Oh, that much?" Bekcy said quickly before she could stop the words from tumbling out. "We'll have to see," she continued and took hold of her little boy's hand who had now lowered his eyes and was staring at the ground in disappointment.

As they walked away hand in hand, the little boy looked up at his mother and said sadly, "Can't we get even a little one, Mother?"

"We must buy something to eat, Jimmy. After that, there won't be enough left," the mother explained apologetically, then bravely added, "but, we'll get something and make a Christmas tree for us, all right, Jimmy?"

"Yes, Mother," the boy replied, trying to sound cheerful so his mother wouldn't feel bad, "and it'll be grand too. I just know it!"

As he turned away, little Jimmy didn't see the tear that issued gently down his mother's cheek, nor could he know the broken heart she suffered in silence because she couldn't give him a better life. Tim could clearly see their poverty and struggles had been a part of their lives for many long years. Yet, Becky radiated an inner strength that seemed to transcend her abject circumstances.

Becky suddenly turned away and began to cough again, but this time it was more severe. She felt blood on her lips and she quickly wiped it away with the back of her hand. After composing herself, Becky turned back to her little boy. And then... *she smiled.*

What? The ground beneath Tim seemed to shift as if something important was happening, but its meaning was just beyond his immediate grasp. Tim just stared, stunned by the scene he was witnessing. Becky's courage and the peaceful acceptance of their hardship, to see it through to the end with dignity, shamed him deeply. Instinctively, he knew he had come to the crux of the ghost's haunting. Tim now realised that on his own he had been unequal to the trials that were a part of his life. And he saw that there was a more powerful song than bitterness and despair. Becky had shown that. In trust and surrender and obedience to God's will, Becky's faith was unshakeable. It was something she had tried to tell him along time ago, but he had not understood.

Becky and Jimmy

The ghost had spoken of a faith that was precious to God, of one that *holds true*. Even with her meagre possessions, her hunger, her misery, and her illness, she walked victorious. His face betrayed him and the heat of his shame rose to his cheeks. Tim's mouth opened and then closed again. He tried to articulate the emotions that flooded him, but couldn't. He desperately wanted to apologise to someone, to anyone. But, in the end, he knew to whom he really wanted to apologise. The unmerited mercy and understanding shown to him was so pure that it staggered him.

And now he needed to answer that mercy — by doing *something*. He couldn't stand still for one more minute, but didn't have any real idea where to start.

"Oh! Mr. Scrooge, what is to become of them? Can't you help them? Isn't there anyone to help them?" Tim cried.

"You can answer that yourself, Tim, if the name *Christmas* means more to you than just a word. Christmas, Tim, more than any other time of the year, is a time when people of good will come together with one common voice of love. It is a charitable time of kindness and forgiving, a benevolent time when men, women, and children willingly soften their hearts, foregoing the self-interests of getting more, and think to share their blessings with their fellow man by giving more. The needs of the poor, whether poor in spirit or in simple necessities, are most visible this time of the year, but they're always there, and we must never turn our eyes from those who need our help.

"God *is* always with us, Tim. He cried with you when you ran down the street. He saw you through the eyes of the beggar you did not help. And He was helping that little girl place the cross in your hand. And He is here... right now! Truly, we are saved only by the grace of God that comes from our faith in Him. That is the gift He gave to us. To all of us. All our journeys, whether easy or difficult, are designed for all of us to come to that revelation if only we could just see it. But, through being saved we become new creatures of God, and by His example, it is our own sacred mission to continue His work. We desire to be His ambassadors here on earth, first with our words about His grace to us all and then by behaving in a manner that is pleasing to Him. God is *watching*... to see what each one of us will do for another... and is glorified by our *actions*.

"Tim, now hear me well. I can no longer help anyone. I am beyond that kind of power to make a difference anymore. Now — it's your turn — to be one of those lights in the dark. It is now up to you and people like you. All of this is yours now, Tim, to remember and carry on...

remember ... *remember* ... *remember* ... " the last of the ghost's words trailed off into an echo as he faded... and then he was gone as a starry Christmas night looked down upon a sleeping Tiny Tim.

The Face of God

STAVE 5

A New Christmas Spirit

Bells! Bells! The clanging was everywhere! Every church bell and all the bells of the city clocks. Even the chimes of the mantlepiece clock downstairs joined the proclamation. Christmas morning! Wonderful Christmas morning! Joyous, joyous Christmas morning!

Tim sat up full in bed, shaken and humbled. For the first time in years, he closed his eyes and truly gave thanks for his many, many blessings. "I'll remember what Christmas means, Mr. Scrooge. Always! And may God forgive me for the time I have wasted." With that pledge made, Tim jumped out of bed to begin his new mission and his new purpose he had accepted from Scrooge's ghost.

"Mother! Father! It's Christmas! It's Christmas! Are you up?" Mrs. Cratchit opened her eyes first and called to Tim from his parent's bedroom. "Tim, in here."

Tim bounced into their bedroom with a bound and again exclaimed, "It's Christmas! It's Christmas!"

His mother and father grinned with surprised joy to see the wonderful change that had come over their boy and immediately jumped out of bed and joined Tim in his celebration, and they all hugged and kissed and laughed and did a jig around and around until Tim remembered Becky and her little boy.

"Becky!" Tim said out loud and ran from the room without any explanation for his actions.

"Who did he say, Love?" Cratchit asked his puzzled wife.

"Becky," she answered quickly. "He said, 'Becky,'" she repeated, trying to make some kind of sense of the name. Then, with a quick meaningful look to Bob, she said, "Did he mean... *his* Becky?"

Meanwhile, Tim was dressing with all the speed at his command, and when he had finished, he ran from the house shouting as he went, "I'll be back, Father! I'll be back, Mother! I'll be back!" his voice getting fainter as he got farther away.

Down he street he ran, going faster than any prudent caution would allow on the slippery snow and ice, down toward the shops that would be open briefly on Christmas morning as a service to their customers' last-minute needs.

As he got nearer to the shopping district, he could hear voices of Christmas carollers singing "♫ *O Come You Christmas Carollers* ♫," then sail right into "♫ *Ring-Ring-Ring The Bells* ♫," and they meant it too, for among them were several good hand bell ringers who rang out with great enthusiasm every time the word 'ring' was mentioned in the Christmas carol, and this happened at the beginning of each verse to the delight of the musicians.

Included in the ranks of these wonderful revellers were men and women, boys and girls, young and old, rich and poor. They were all there with faces laughing and voices singing out their praises for the hopeful promise of the day and for all their blessings.

As Tim came into view of the shops, he could see that the poulterer's was open and that would be his first stop. He was surprised to find so many people there who hadn't picked up their bird the day before and had to wait in line to order. Finally, when the poulterer said, "Next,"

Tim stepped forward and, with a twinkle in his eye, greeted the man warmly, "A happy, happy Christmas to you, Tom!"

Christmas Morning

"M-merry Christmas to yourself, Tim," Tom sputtered back, surprised to see him there.

"A goose, I think," said Tim, almost as much to himself as to Tom. "Yes, a Christmas goose," he added now with certainty. "Not too large a one, one that would be enough for say, three."

"I thought your mother already picked up your goose, Tim," the poulterer returned. "Didn't she get it yesterday?"

"This isn't for our family," Tim explained with a smile Tom recognised as that of someone purchasing a gift.

Searching for a goose now with the squinting eye of a master poulterer, Tom selected a particularly handsome bird, round and plump to behold, and then presented the long-necked fowl for Tim to inspect.

Tim examined the bird with great deliberation not wanting to appear as if he had never done this sort of thing before and then, in his best voice of calm authority, answered, "Good choice, Tom."

"That'll be one and six, Tim," the smiling man said and exchanged the bird for the payment.

"A Merry Christmas, Tom," Tim wished him again, "and all of your family too," he remembered, and he and the goose hurried out to their next stop.

Just down the street was a toy shop and this is where he now headed with great expectations. *Tinkle, tinkle,* went the little bell above the toy shop door as he entered and joined the merry band of last-minute Christmas shoppers already there. He quickly inspected many things with his experienced eye, and he did have one, for hadn't he, himself, been a boy and the owner of such things?

"Yes," he said to himself pleased and satisfied with his selection each time he added something to the growing hoard of toys under his arm.

Finally, he had what he wanted, paid for it, and left the shop with a definite destination in mind. Briskly he walked now, loaded down with his wonderful burdens, determined to keep the promise he had made. In minutes he was coming upon a man selling Christmas trees on a corner.

"Something in a tree ?" the man asked as Tim approached, his voice rising at the end of the sentence to show he meant it to be a question.

"Yes," replied Tim with an absolute tone that told this merchant that this was, indeed, a sure sale. Much care was needed, Tim thought, to choose just the right tree for this special occasion, just the right tree for these special people.

"This one," Tim said quickly, pointing with his elbow to the tallest tree there.

"A good one, I'd say too, sir!" the tree seller voiced his approval and moved quickly to clinch the deal. Tim paid the man just as quickly and then walked toward another man sitting atop a coach a short way up the street.

"I say there, coachman! Are you for hire or have you been taken?" Tim called out with hopeful expectation.

"I'm for hire, sir!" the coachman called back with the same hopeful expectation at the thought of gaining a paying customer. Seeing that Tim had too much to carry — and not enough arms — the coachman quickly vacated his seat on the coach and scurried to Tim's aid. Then, after all the presents were put into the coach and the tall Christmas tree was tied securely to the back, the coachman remounted his seat with Tim at his side and asked, "Where to, sir?"

Tim stared blankly down the street and then, with puzzled reservation, answered, "I'm not sure!" All he knew was that Becky lived in a very poor part of the city and that he had seen a name on a street sign. For anxious moments, Tim frantically searched his mind to remember the name on the sign near Becky's house from the haunting the night before. Then, with a burst of excitement at remembering, he shouted, "Herald Street! Do you know where there's a Herald Street?

The coachman drew his finger to his mouth as he pondered the question with great effort, not wanting to lose his fare — especially since they were loaded and ready to go — but, mostly because he could see how much it meant to Tim. Then, with great jubilation ringing in his voice, he proclaimed, "I remember now, sir!" and released the brake with a flourish.

Off down the street they then went at a gallop with eager expectation glowing in all four of their smiling faces — even the horses were smiling — with a new hope in their hearts at the prospect of finding the elusive Herald Street.

Finding Becky

After what seemed like an eternity to Tim, the coach slowed and the driver started cautiously through this older part of the city, block by block. The area was so bleak that the only bits of evidence that life existed here at all were the black smoke belching from every chimney and two scraggly cats, thin as wafers, out upon a morning's foraging for their breakfast.

"Are you sure it's this way?" Tim asked nervously as success seemed a more distant promise with each street they crossed.

"I was almost sure it was here somewhere, sir," the coachman answered now with an apologetic tone and words that sounded not sure at all.

As they drew within sight of the last street sign, Tim jumped to his feet with unbridled emotion, shouting, "That's it! Herald Street! We've found it!"

"I see it, sir!" the coachman shouted back with the same uncontrolled joy that Tim had shown in finding the street. Turning the corner now, they started down Herald Street with shabby buildings lining both sides for as far as the eye could see.

"Which place is it, sir?" the coachman asked brightly, still bubbling joyfully at their good luck.

"I don't know!" Tim answered with frustration showing in his voice. "I've only been there once before. Drive down the street slowly and I'll try to find something that looks familiar."

Slowly, the coach moved now with Tim agonisingly scanning every window, every street lamp, anything he might be able to recognise, yet nothing looked familiar. Up ahead now, Tim could see that Herald Street came to a dead end just beyond the corner, and his heart fell at the thought of not finding Becky and Jimmy after he had been so sure he would.

"That looks like the end up there, sir," the coachman said with sadness apparent in his voice.

But then, as they crossed the last corner and their last chance, Tim looked down the street they were crossing and a little boy with a tattered old coat came out of the door of the second house from the corner.

"Stop!" cried Tim with such exuberance that his voice carried all the way to the little boy's house and his mother came out to see what was happening.

Jumping from the seat of the coach now with total disregard of the slippery snow and ice, Tim rushed toward the pretty young lady without any thought of explanation for his presence and, reaching out his hand to her, thankfully called out her name, "B-e-c-k-y..."

For a moment, Becky just stood there looking at Tim with a searching look of unrecognition, for Tim also had changed over the years. Then slowly, an expression of astonished surprise crossed her delicate face. As she nervously smoothed a wisp of her hair back from her forehead, she said in an almost unbelieving voice, "Tim?" Tim could only reply by nodding his head, his heart was so full of joy at the sight of Becky.

"I've come to find you, Becky," he finally managed to say. "Thank God, I have!"

Becky held out her hand to him and he took it tenderly in both of his in a gentle, caring way. For a few moments, the two of them just stood there looking at each other without speaking. Then, Becky said in a soft voice, "I've often thought of you, Tim."

> *Except for the times I breathe in,*
> *I think of you only when I breathe out...*

Tim squeezed her small hand even tighter as his reply and then looked down at the little boy by her side. "And this is Jimmy," Tim said softly.

"Yes, but how did you —"

She wasn't able to complete her question because Tim interrupted with, "Somebody told me... a friend," as he placed his hand on the little boy's head and gently caressed his hair.

At this same time for just an instant, Tim saw Scrooge's ghost standing across the street smiling at him and holding up three fingers. Tim smiled in reply for he understood now who the three people were the ghost needed to help.

Tim now turned to Becky and asked the most important question of his life: "I want to help you, Becky. Please, let me?"

"Oh, Tim, Jimmy and I can get by, honestly," Becky replied, embarrassed by what she must look like to Tim.

"I know you can, Becky. But, I can't... without you! I love you!" Crying and laughing at the same time, Tim exclaimed, "I feel as if I've been asleep for a long, long time, unseeing and unaware. But now, I'm awake! I feel alive again! And I mustn't miss one more minute of it all!"

Tim looked deep into Becky's beautiful soft brown eyes. "I have so much to learn," Tim now pleaded with his whole heart and soul. "Will... *you help me?*"

Becky's surprised smile at Tim's wonderful words and her gentle squeeze of his hand were all the answers Tim would ever need. He then looked over to find little Jimmy standing by the coach starring at him with anxiety and uncertainty on his small face and quickly called, "Jimmy! Come on!"

"Me?" Jimmy shouted back, pointing to his chest. "You want me?" He slowly walked toward where Tim and Becky were standing together holding hands.

"Of course, I do," Tim answered. "We need you, Jimmy! We're going to be a family now — that is, if you wish it."

Jimmy looked at the smile his mother had for Tim, and then he looked up for a long moment into Tim's eyes without any expression, searching to see if Tim really meant what he had said. Slowly, Jimmy relaxed and smiled as he reached for Tim's extended hand and placed his on top.

"Oh, dearest, dearest Becky, the merriest of Christmases ever!" Tim wished her with all the devotion of his heart as he pulled her close to him. "And God bless us, everyone!"

And so it was then, on that good day of the year, Christmas Day, three people found each other and received the greatest gift in the world: love. May that truly be a gift we bestow from each of us, one to the other.

The Reunion

Norman Whaler

Songs of the

Carollers

Have a Very-Very Merry-Merry Christmas
Norman Whaler

HAVE A VERY-VERY MERRY-MERRY CHRISTMAS
WITH LOTS OF CHRISTMAS CHEER
AND ALL THE THINGS
THAT CHRISTMAS BRINGS
THIS SEASON OF THE YEAR

HAVE A VERY-VERY MERRY-MERRY CHRISTMAS
THE BEST ONE THERE CAN BE
AND THE SAME THING GOES
FOR ALL OF THOSE
AROUND YOUR CHRISTMAS TREE

AND WHILE I'M MAKING WISHES
OF THINGS I'D LIKE TO SEE
I'LL WISH A MERRY CHRISTMAS-TO ME

HAVE A VERY-VERY MERRY-MERRY CHRISTMAS
AND IF MY WISH COMES TRUE
YOU'LL HAVE A MERRY CHRISTMAS NOW
AND HAVE ONE NEXT YEAR TOO

Have a Very-Very Merry-Merry Christmas

Christmas All Year' Round
Norman Whaler

EVERYTHING THAT I SEE
IS SAYING TO ME
CHRISTMAS TIME IS GETTING NEAR
AND BEFORE YOU KNOW
THERE'LL BE PLENTY OF SNOW
AND SLEIGH BELLS
AND THOUGHTS OF GOOD CHEER

ALL THE BRIGHT LIGHTS AGLOW
WHEREVER I GO
REMIND ME OF CHRISTMASES PAST
AND THE CAROLS BEING SUNG
WHILE THE STOCKINGS ARE HUNG
MAKE ME WISH
CHRISTMAS COULD LAST

'CAUSE IT'S THE TIME OF THE YEAR
WHEN CHRISTMAS IS NEAR
THAT ALL THE WORLD SEEMS RIGHT
SO, PUT A LOG ON THE FIRE
SO, THE FLAME WILL GO HIGHER
AND MAKE THE YULETIDE BRIGHT

OH, I JUST LOVE TO SEE
A GREEN CHRISTMAS TREE
AND FOLKS ON THEIR WAY HOMEWARD
BOUND
AND EVERYTIME I SEE
A CHRISTMAS TREE
I WISH IT COULD BE CHRISTMAS
ALL YEAR'ROUND

Christmas All Year 'Round

Moderato

WHALER

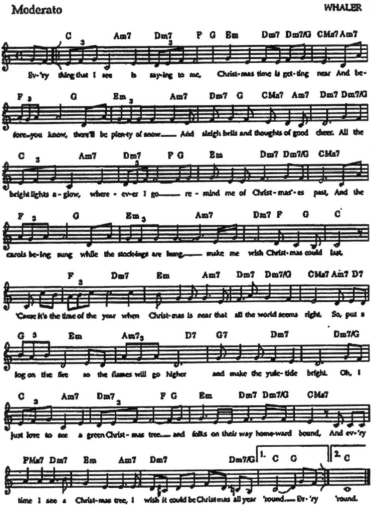

Ring-Ring-Ring The Bells
Norman Whaler

RING-RING-RING THE BELLS
TOLL THEM FOR ALL TO HEAR
RING, RING, RING THE BELLS
TELL THEM THE CHILD IS HERE
BRIGHTEST STAR ABOVE
GUIDE THE WAY TONIGHT
TO THE PLACE IN BETHLEHEM
BATHED IN HOLY LIGHT

RING-RING-RING THE BELLS
TO GIVE THE WORLD A SIGN
OF THE VIRGIN BIRTH
OF THE CHILD DEVINE
BLESSED SON OF GOD
BRINGING US HIS LOVE
HOLY LIGHT SHINES DOWN ON HIM
FROM THE STAR ABOVE

RING-RING-RING THE BELLS
TELL OF HIS HOLY GRACE
WISE MEN JOURNEY TO
LOOK ON HIS HEAVENLY FACE
BORN THE KING OF KINGS
SACRED HEART SO PURE
GOD THE FATHER GAVE HIS SON
ETERNAL LOVE TO INSURE

RING-RING-RING THE BELLS
WHILE ANGELS' VOICES SING
OF JOY TO THE WORLD
OUR SAVIOR'S BIRTH WILL BRING
HOLY, HOLY CHILD
HEAR THE ANGELS SAY
JESUS CHRIST, THE PRINCE OF PEACE
IS BORN TODAY

Ring-Ring-Ring The Bells

Rhythmically (like tolling bells)

WHALER

O Come, You Christmas Carollers
Norman Whaler

O COME, YOU CHRISTMAS CAROLLERS
SING THE NEWS TO EVERY EAR
HAS COME FOR US A SAVIOUR
BORN TODAY SO SMALL AND PURE

O SEE HIM IN HIS MANGER
MARY'S CARING FOR HER CHILD
AND JOSEPH'S NEAR SO HE'LL PROTECT
CHOSEN MOTHER, HOLY CHILD

LISTEN, ALL YOU PEOPLE, TO THE MESSAGE
THAT THE CAROLLERS SING
THEY ARE TELLING OF THE JOY
THIS LITTLE BABE WILL BRING

SO COME, YOU CHRISTMAS CAROLLERS
SING THE NEWS YOU'VE COME TO SING
ITS GLORY TO OUR SAVIOUR
JESUS CHRIST, THE NEWBORN KING

O Come You Christmas Carolers

O Holy Night

Adolphe Charles Adams

Christmas Day in the Morning

(I Saw Three Ships)

Author Unknown

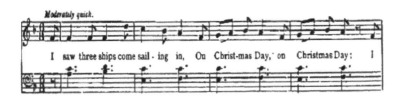

I saw three ships come sail - ing in, On Christ-mas Day, on Christmas Day;

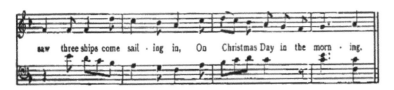

saw three ships come sail - ing in, On Christmas Day in the morn - ing.

2. And what was in those ships all three
On Christmas Day, on Christmas Day;
And what was in those ships all three
On Christmas Day in the morning?

3. Our Saviour Christ and His lady
On Christmas Day, on Christmas Day;
Our Saviour Christ and His lady
On Christmas Day in the morning.

4. Pray whither sailed those ships all three
On Christmas Day, on Christmas Day;
Pray whither sailed those ships all three
On Christmas Day in the morning?

5. O they sailed into Bethlehem
On Christmas Day, on Christmas Day;
O they sailed into Bethlehem
On Christmas Day in the morning.

6. And all the bells on earth shall ring
On Christmas Day, on Christmas Day;
And all the bells on earth shall ring
On Christmas Day in the morning.

7. And all the angels in Heaven shall sing
On Christmas Day, on Christmas Day;
And all the angels in Heaven shall sing
On Christmas Day in the morning.

8. And all the souls on earth shall sing
On Christmas Day, on Christmas Day;
And all the souls on earth shall sing
On Christmas Day in the morning.

9. Then let us all rejoice amain
On Christmas Day, on Christmas Day;
Then let us all rejoice amain
On Christmas day in the morning.

Norman Whaler

We Wish You A Merry Christmas

Now bring us figgy pudding
Now bring us figgy pudding
And a cup of good cheer!
Glad tidings we bring
To you and your kin;
Glad tidings for Christmas
And a happy New Year!

We won't go until we get some
We won't go until we get some
We won't go until we get some
So bring it out here!
Glad tidings we bring
To you and your kin;
Glad tidings for Christmas
And a happy New Year!

We wish you a Merry Christmas
We wish you a Merry Christmas
We wish you a Merry Christmas
And a happy New Year.

JOY TO THE WORLD

(ANTIOCH)

Isaac Watts, 1709

G. F. Handel

3. No more let sin and sorrow grow,
Nor thorns infest the ground;
He comes to make his blessings flow
Far as the curse is found.

4. He rules the world with truth and grace,
And makes the nations prove
The glories of his righteousness,
And wonders of his love.

God rest you merry gentlemen

An Additional verse may be sung as follows:

God bless the ruler of this house,
And send him long to reign.
And many a happy Christmas
May live to see again
Among your friends * and kindred,
That live both far and near,
And God send you a happy new year

*It is thought that the word "friends" was used in
London streets in place of "friends"

O COME, ALL YE FAITHFUL
(ADESTE FIDELES)

Anon. (Latin, 17th Cent.)
Tr. F. Oakeley, 1841

Melody by John Reading, 1677-1764

1. 'O come, all ye faith - ful, joy - ful and tri - um - phant,
2. Sing, choirs of an - gels, sing in ex - ul - ta - tion,
3. Yes, Lord, we greet thee, born for our sal - va - tion,

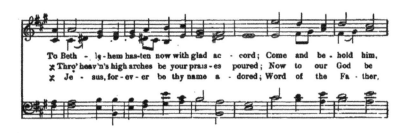

To Beth - le - hem has-ten now with glad ac - cord; Come and be - hold him,
Thro' heav'n's high arches be your prais - es poured; Now to our God be
Je - sus, for - ev - er be thy name a - dored; Word of the Fa - ther,

After each verse

born the King of an - gels; O come, let us a - dore him,
glo - ry in the high - est; O come, let us a - dore him,
now in flesh ap - pear - ing; O come, let us a - dore him,

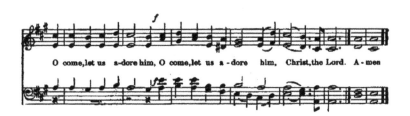

O come,let us a-dore him, O come,let us a - dore him, Christ,the Lord. A - men

Deck the Hall

words: traditional English

tune: *Nos Galan*, traditional Welsh

The First Nowell

traditional English, 18th cent.

traditional English, 17th cent.
harm. John Stainer, alt.

Illustration Credits

Cover art, Stewart Sherwood
Tiny Tim Cratchit, Norman Whaler
"♫ Have a Very-Very Merry-Merry Christmas ♫"
Stewart Sherwood
Becky and Tim, victorianpicturelibrary.com, uk
The Storm, dreamstime.com
"A bit of Holly for your Christmas?"
victorianpicturelibrary.com, uk
Praying for a Miracle, victorianpicturelibrary.com, uk
"Tiiiiiimm...", Norman Whaler
Scrooge's Ghost, coolclips.com
Old Scrooge, Ggchristmas, clipartof.com
Melted Candle, Getty Images, istockphoto.com
Becky and Jimmy, Artist Ley
The Face of God, fotosearch.com
Christmas Morning, marg.com.uk
Finding Becky, J. L.Williams, webweaver.nu
The Reunion, 123rf.com
Victorian Christmas Carollers, clipartpal.com
Songs of the Carollers, clipartbest.com

Traditional Christmas Carol Sheet Music —
cantadomino.org, janwoltesr.nl,
christmascarolmusic.org, cantorion.org
pianoandsynth.com, lilypond.org

Acknowledgement

TWINKLE, TWINKLE, LITTLE STAR
Nursery Rhyme Anne
and Jane Taylor
London, 1806

Norman Whaler is from Grosse Pointe, MI, and lives in the USA. He is a member of SCBWI (Society of Children's Book Writers and Illustrators), ACFW (American Christian Fiction Writers), and CIPA, IAN, and IBPA associations. This Christmas book is dedicated to his late wife and love, Patricia Aybar Whaler.

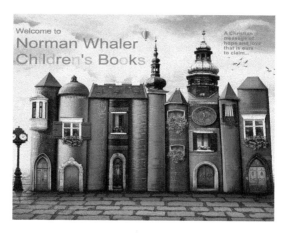

normanwhaler.com

Norman Whaler (father), classical pianist and composer, and also from Grosse Pointe, wrote new Christmas carols for this book adding to the beautiful backdrop of a Christmas in Victorian England. He lived the spirit of Christmas every day. He has since passed in Dec 2011.

Other Books By Norman Whaler

Audio Book

Spanish

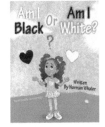

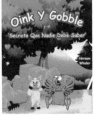

Merry

Christmas